CALUMET CITY PUBLIC LIBRARY

3 1613 00362 5459

W9-CEI-109

J
582.16
BOD

Pebble® Plus

Plant Parts
Leaves

by Vijaya Khisty Bodach

Consulting Editor: Gail Saunders-Smith, PhD

Consultant: Judson R. Scott, Current President
American Society of Consulting Arborists

Capstone
press®

Mankato, Minnesota

CALUMET CITY PUBLIC LIBRARY

Pebble Plus is published by Capstone Press,
151 Good Counsel Drive, P.O. Box 669, Mankato, Minnesota 56002.
www.capstonepress.com

Copyright © 2007 by Capstone Press. All rights reserved.
No part of this publication may be reproduced in whole or in part, or stored in a retrieval system, or
transmitted in any form or by any means, electronic, mechanical, photocopying, recording, or otherwise,
without written permission of the publisher. For information regarding permission, write to Capstone Press,
151 Good Counsel Drive, P.O. Box 669, Dept. R, Mankato, Minnesota 56002.
Printed in the United States of America

1 2 3 4 5 6 11 10 09 08 07 06

Library of Congress Cataloging-in-Publication Data
Bodach, Vijaya Khisty.
    Leaves / by Vijaya Khisty Bodach.
    p. cm.—(Pebble plus. Plant parts)
    Summary: "Simple text and photographs present the leaves of plants, how they grow, and their
uses"—Provided by publisher.
    Includes bibliographical references (p. 23) and index.
    ISBN-13: 978-0-7368-6344-5 (hardcover)
    ISBN-10: 0-7368-6344-3 (hardcover)
    ISBN-13: 978-0-7368-7545-5 (softcover pbk.)
    ISBN-10: 0-7368-7545-X (softcover pbk.)
    1. Leaves—Juvenile literature. I. Title. II. Series.
QK649.B66 2007
575.5'7—dc22   2006000992

Editorial Credits
Sarah L. Schuette, editor; Jennifer Bergstrom, designer; Kelly Garvin, photo researcher/photo editor

Photo Credits
Capstone Press/Karon Dubke, cover, 5
Dwight R. Kuhn, 14–15, 16–17, 22 (seed, seedling)
James P. Rowan, 6–7, 20–21
Peter Arnold/Ed Reschke, 18–19
Richard Hamilton Smith, 8–9
Shutterstock/Mr. Zap, 12–13; Romeo Koitmae, 1; Shonn, 22 (tree); WizData Inc., 11

Note to Parents and Teachers

The Plant Parts set supports national science standards related to identifying plant
parts and the diversity and interdependence of life. This book describes and illustrates
leaves. The images support early readers in understanding the text. The repetition of
words and phrases helps early readers learn new words. This book also introduces early
readers to subject-specific vocabulary words, which are defined in the Glossary section.
Early readers may need assistance to read some words and to use the Table of Contents,
Glossary, Read More, Internet Sites, and Index sections of the book.

Table of Contents

Plants Need Leaves

Leaves grow from
the stems of plants.
Most leaves are green.

Leaves make food
for the whole plant.
They use water, air,
and sunlight
to make the food.

Veins inside leaves
bring the food to the stem.
Stems carry the food
to the rest of the plant.

Leaves give off oxygen

when they make food.

We breathe oxygen.

All Kinds of Leaves

Thin pine tree leaves

look like needles.

They stay green

all year long.

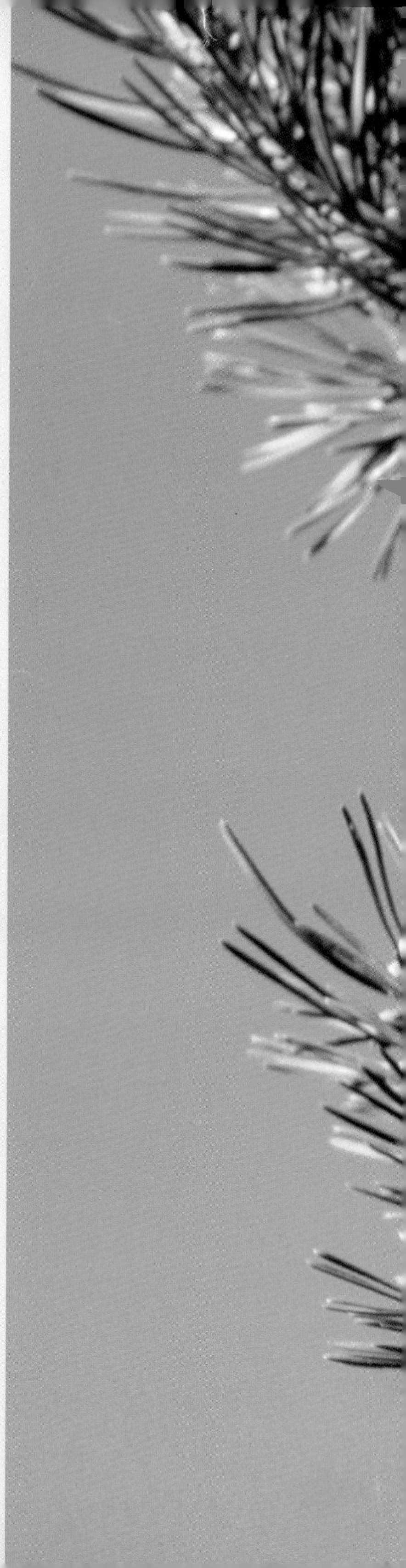

31813 00362 5459

CALUMET CITY PUBLIC LIBRARY

13

Broad maple leaves

turn orange and yellow

in autumn.

They fall off the tree.

New leaves grow in spring.

Eating Leaves

Lettuce leaves make
a tasty salad.
Each head of lettuce
has layers of leaves.

Giraffes eat only leaves.
They spend most of the day
biting leaves off tree tops.

Wonderful Leaves

Broad or narrow,

soft or fuzzy,

leaves help plants stay alive.

Parts of a Maple Tree

leaves

seed

leaves

stem

stem

Glossary

oxygen—a colorless gas in the air; people and animals breathe oxygen.

stem—the long main part of a plant that makes leaves; food made by leaves moves through stems to the rest of the plant.

veins—the small tubes inside a leaf; veins carry food and water.

Read More

Farndon, John. *Leaves.* World of Plants. San Diego: Blackbirch Press, 2005.

Freeman, Marcia S. *What Plant Is This?* Everything Science. Vero Beach, Fla.: Rourke, 2005.

Mattern, Joanne. *How Pine Trees Grow.* How Plants Grow. Milwaukee: Weekly Reader, 2006.

Index

Word Count: 130
Grade: 1
Early-Intervention Level: 15

Internet Sites

FactHound offers a safe, fun way to find Internet sites related to this book. All of the sites on FactHound have been researched by our staff.

Here's how:

1. Visit *www.facthound.com*

2. Choose your grade level.

3. Type in this book ID **0736863443** for age-appropriate sites. You may also browse subjects by clicking on letters, or by clicking on pictures and words.

4. Click on the **Fetch It** button.

Facthound will fetch the best sites for you!